The Dukeries

Clumber, Rufford
Thoresby and Wor

on old picture p

Philip Jones and Michael Riley

WELBECK

1. View of the east front from across the Shrubbery Lake. Little survives of the Premonstratensian Abbey (founded 1153), the present buildings being mainly Victorian. The Abbey is now used as an Army sixth-form college. 'Phototype' postcard no. 80546 published by Valentine & Sons.

Designed and Published by
Reflections of a Bygone Age
Keyworth, Nottingham
1993

ISBN 0 946245 71 1

Printed by
Adlard Print and Typesetting Services,
Ruddington, Notts.

Front cover: Clumber House
Back cover (top): the east front of Rufford depicted on a Frederick Hartmann card. The large bay almost half-way along this side housed the grand staircase.
(bottom): Welbeck Abbey

2. The west or Oxford Wing, refurbished by Henrietta, Countess of Oxford, between 1741 and 1752, was gutted by fire on 5th October 1900. It was rebuilt by Sir Ernest George, who was also responsible for extensive improvements to the exterior and interior of the Abbey. 'Woodbury' series card no. 2520, posted to Wrexham in August 1906. *"Perhaps you already know that the Duke of Portland lives here,"* wrote the sender.

3. The entrance hall. A Flemish tapestry illustrating Charles II on horseback and a fireplace attributed to Thomas Carter (1744) are the notable features on this photographic card no.6621 published by G.W. Wilson.

INTRODUCTION

The Dukeries is a large tract of land in the northern part of Nottinghamshire, which at one time was owned by four ducal families – the Dukes of Portland (Welbeck Abbey), Norfolk (Worksop Manor), Newcastle (Clumber) and Kingston (Thoresby). The word 'Dukery' was first coined in the 18th century, but came into popular use in the 19th century during the parliamentary debates on reform in 1831 and 1832.

Rufford Abbey, the seat of the Savile family, although never owned by a duke, is usually included in The Dukeries since it is geographically in the same area. All the estates are within a four mile radius of each other. It is the existence of these estates which has helped to preserve much of Sherwood Forest from complete destruction.

Unfortunately, the grandeur of these country estates has disappeared forever. Clumber House was demolished in 1938 and Rufford Abbey partially demolished in 1956, although their parks are open for the public to enjoy. Whilst Welbeck Abbey and Worksop Manor remain firmly in private hands and closed to the public, the fate of Thoresby Hall at present seems unclear.

This book does not set out to relate the history of The Dukeries – that has already been admirably done elsewhere. What it hopes to do, through the medium of the picture postcard, is to re-capture some of the splendour of Nottinghamshire's ducal houses that has gone forever.

Picture postcards were first published in this country in 1894 but it was not until 1902 that the Post Office allowed the message to be written on the back alongside the address. This lead to a boom in picture postcard production and useage – the "Golden Age" of postcards – which lasted up to the end of the First World War (1918).

This book draws on a wealth of material available, from national publishers such as Valentine, W.H. Smith and G.W. Wilson, to more local ones such as Ezra Taylor of Worksop and Edgar Welchman of Retford. We hope our choice of cards succeeds in conveying the glory and splendour of the Nottinghamshire country house as it was in its "Golden Age".

Philip Jones
Michael Riley
March 1993

4. Only the plaster fan-vault and upper part of the fireplace by Christopher Richardson (1748-1751) survived the alterations to the Gothic Hall carried out by Sir Ernest George in 1900-1902. Card published by Ezra Taylor & Son of Worksop.

5. State Drawing Room. 'Kingsway' Real Photo series card no. S6242, published by W.H. Smith & Son, showing French tapestries by Gobelin (1783).

6. The large representation of a swan on the Axminster carpet gave this room the name of Swan Drawing Room. 'Kingsway' series card no. 2559, posted in April 1908.

7. The Titchfield Library. Part of the old riding school was converted into a library in 1873 from designs by Sedding and Wilson. 'Kingsway' card.

8. A collection of British birds was housed in one of a number of rooms built underground by the 5th Duke of Portland. These rooms had the advantage of being warm in winter and cool in summer. Photographic card no. 9480 published by G.W. Wilson.

9. The underground ballroom, used as a picture gallery, was reputedly the largest and most magnificent private room in England, measuring 160 feet by 64 feet. Pierced by 27 octagonal skylights in three rows, it was illuminated at night with the aid of 18 glass chandeliers. 'Kingsway' series card no. S6222, posted at Nottingham in September 1914.

10. The chapel, formally opened in December 1892, was designed by the architect John B. Sedding and completed after his death by his pupil Henry Wilson. The Ionic columns are of red marble mottled with grey, and the sumptuous bronze lectern in the foreground was designed by Wilson himself. Card issued by the London Stores, Langwith.

11. The north-east terrace with tea house to the left is depicted in this postcard by Ezra Taylor & Son, posted from Whitwell in August 1912.

12. The lake, formed originally by damming up a brook, was deepened and extended by Humphry Repton in 1789, and is over 3 miles in length. Beyond the lake is the deer park with a circumference of about 10 miles. Phototype card no. 80544, published by Valentine & Sons.

13. The Italianate sunken rose garden, with wooden pavilion and pergolas, formed part of the extensive pleasure grounds covering over 50 acres. Card issued by the London Stores, Langwith.

14. The new riding school, 385 feet long, 104 feet wide and 51 feet high, was reputedly second only in size to that at Vienna. The exterior walls were built of stone and a semi-circular roof of glass and iron, supported by 48 cast-iron columns. 'Kingsway' series card no. 2322.

15. The laundry, built in 1861 by C. & A. Dennett at a cost of £2,180 16s 10d, is featured on this 'Kingsway' series card no. 2591, posted to Buxton in August 1908.

16. These six almshouses, known as The Winnings, were built by the 6th Duke of Portland for the benefit of the poor and to commemorate the success of his race-horses in the years 1888, 1889 and 1890. Card issued by the London Stores, Langwith, and posted at Oldham, Lancashire, in September 1930.

17. Another card in W.H. Smith's 'Kingsway' series (no. S4871) showing the Post Office at Welbeck, completed about 1861 by C. & A. Dennett, using local stone from the 5th Duke's own quarry.

18. The 5th Duke of Portland built miles of underground passages and rooms. One tunnelled carriageway enabled him to drive from the Abbey to the edge of the park without being seen. Valentine series card no. 80542.

19. One of 40 to 50 lodges built on the estate, all in neo-Tudor style and of Steetley stone. These main entrance gates, more usually known as the Lion Gates, were built in 1894 for the 6th Duke of Portland. Valentine card, posted at Sutton-in-Ashfield in May 1905.

20. This Russian log cabin was used by the Dukes as a shooting box. Card no. 610 published by R. Sneath of Sheffield.

WORKSOP MANOR

21. The original Elizabethan manor house, completed by Bess of Hardwick c.1585, was one of the largest in England, with over 500 rooms. This building was destroyed by fire in October 1761. Card published by John William Caseldine of Worksop and printed in Germany.

22. In 1840 the 12th Duke of Norfolk sold the estate to the 4th Duke of Newcastle, who partially demolished what had been rebuilt by James Paine after the fire of 1761. A portion which remained was converted into this modest residence. 'Kingsway' card no. 2534, sent to Sedbergh in May 1913.

23. This solid stone screen with Doric columns and triumphal arch was built by James Paine to conceal the stable court and also to make the house look larger when seen from the park. 'Sherwood' series card published by J.W. Caseldine.

24. The dining-room of Worksop Manor in the early years of the 20th century. The house and part of the estate was owned at this time by Sir John Robinson, founder of the Home Brewery. 'Kingsway' card no. 2543.

25. Castle Farm, half-a-mile to the south-east of the house, was designed in 1758 by the Duchess of Norfolk. It is now the home of a member of the Farr family, the present owners of the Worksop estate. Thomas Ratcliffe's 'Dukery' series card, posted to Sheffield in March 1906.

CLUMBER

26. The house at Clumber was built c.1760-1770 by Stephen Wright and enlarged in 1857 by Sir Charles Barry, architect of the Houses of Parliament. 'Hop Pole' series card published by Frederick Willman of Mansfield, proprietor of the *Mansfield Chronicle.*

27. The oldest (central) part of the house was rebuilt by the younger Charles Barry, after a disastrous fire on 26th March 1879 had destroyed 20 of the 105 rooms. Apart from a small fragment the house was completely demolished in 1938. The park is now the property of the National Trust. Anonymously-published card posted from Retford in March 1909.

28. The east front, Clumber. Rooms along this side of the house included the billiard room, east drawing room, study and reading room. Postcard no. 146 published by William Edgar Welchman of Retford.

29. The state drawing room was re-decorated in the 1860s for the visit of the Prince of Wales. The walls were hung with a rich cream satin damask. The gilded cornices and other carved work came from the Doge's Palace at Venice. 'Kingsway' card no. S4211 published by W.H. Smith & Sons.

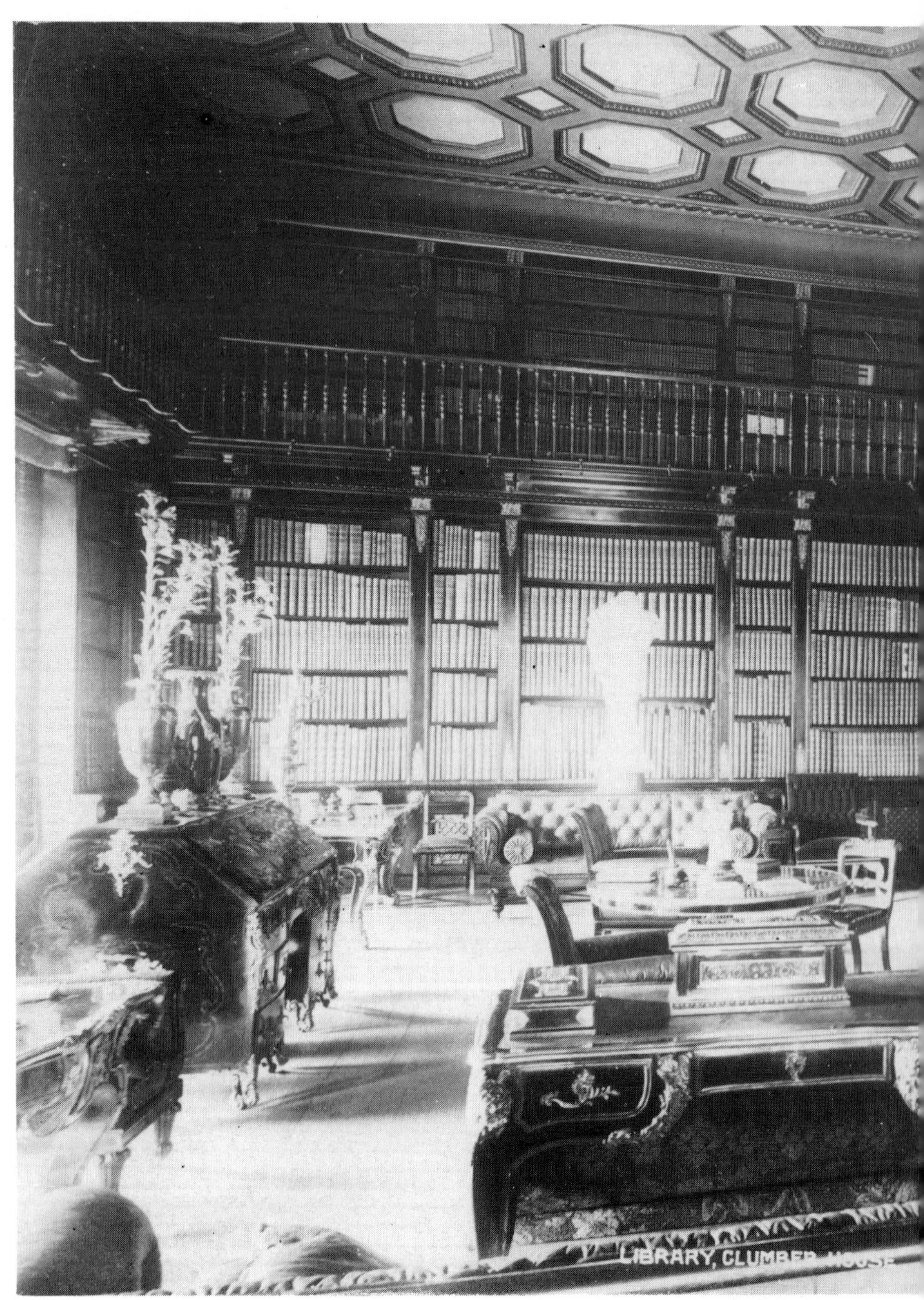

30. The library was fitted with Spanish mahogany and cont
Caxton and other early printers. Photographic card no. 8069

me 50,000 volumes, including many rare editions by
ed by G.W. Wilson.

31. A notable feature of the billiard room was a panelled oak dado. The walls were hung with a large collection of historical portraits, including works by Gainsborough and Holbein. Photographic card no. 9469 published by G.W. Wilson.

32. The main terrace garden was created about 1828 in the Italian style and contained some decorative vases and urns brought from Worksop Manor. Just visible, on the right, is a white marble fountain which was cut from one solid block weighing 50 tons. Card no. 1295 published by R. Sneath of Sheffield.

33. The descent of the terraces to the serpentine lake, which was begun in 1774 and completed in 1789. The Park beyond comprised about 4,000 acres. Valentine's series card no. 22476, posted to Whaley Bridge in December 1907.

34. Boats were very fashionable on ducal lakes. Clumber had several vessels, including the *"Salamanca"*, named after Wellington's victory in 1812, and a 40-ton frigate called the *"Lincoln"*. The latter was burned at its mooring by children about 1940. Anonymously-published photographic card.

35. The formal garden at Clumber ended with the Lincoln Terrace, a straight walk o about a quarter of a mile along the side of the lake. The walk was accentuated by fur- ther vases and urns, and a row of Irish yews. Photographic card no. 6690 published by G.W. Wilson.

6690. G.W.W.

36. The Church of St. Mary the Virgin, still standing today, was built between 1886 and 1889 to designs by Bodley and Garner. The central tower, with spire, is 180 feet high. Card by Ezra Taylor of Worksop.

37. The church is built of white Steetley stone faced with red Runcorn stone dressings. The sanctuary is paved with black and white marble, and the high altar, tabernacle and altar shelf are in white alabaster. 'Kingsway' postcard no.2341, posted from Mansfield in November 1908.

38. The fine three-arched classical stone bridge built originally by Fuller White in 1763 is shown in this 'Art' series card.

39. The Lime Tree Avenue, one of the finest in Europe, stretches for three miles to Apleyhead Lodge. The trees were planted in double rows on each side of the road about 1840. Valentine's XL series card no. 22760.

40. A Bullnose Morris passing through the triumphal arch of Apleyhead Lodge (built about 1787). 'Colonial' series card no.2110, published by C. & A.G. Lewis of Nottingham.

41. A castellated archway and lodge completed about 1789 are featured on this 'Kingsway' card no. S4965.

THORESBY

42. The west front of Thoresby. The present building, the third Thoresby Hall to be erected in the Park, was built in Elizabethan style between 1864 and 1875, after designs by Anthony Salvin. 'Woodbury' series card no. 2516 published by Eyre & Spottiswoode of London.

43. View of the house from the south terrace. The main fronts were the east (entrance front) measuring 180 feet long, and this, the south or drawing-room side, measuring 182 feet long. 'Art' series card posted from Mansfield in July 1907.

44. Deer have always been a feature of the Park, ever since it was enclosed in the 17th century by William Pierrepont, fourth Earl of Kingston. Anonymously-published photographic card.

45. Visitors approached the house through these elaborate wrought-iron gates by Brawn and Downing of Birmingham. Great Central Railway card no. 2438 sold at Worksop Station, the nearest connection to Thoresby.

46. Originally known as the Edwinstowe Gate, the late 18th/early 19th century Buck Gates have good examples of 18th century lead statues of bucks. Valentine's series card no. 22485.

47. St. John the Evangelist Church, a short distance to the south-east of the house, was built in 1876 after designs by Anthony Salvin. The building replaced an older church, whose registers date back to 1528. Anonymously-published card sent from Beighton, near Sheffield, to Ilfracombe in July 1910.

48. The Grand Drawing Room, also known as the Blue Drawing Room from the pale blue silk damask with which the walls are covered. Two marble chimneypieces in this room have figures sitting on canted angles, representing the four seasons.

OOM
ORES

49. The Georgian Bridge across the River Meden has always been popular with visitors because of its woodland setting. Card published by Ezra Taylor of Worksop.

RUFFORD

50. Founded as a Cistercian monastery about 1146, Rufford was granted after its dissolution (1537) to the Earls of Shrewbury, who demolished some of the monastic buildings and created a modest country house out of the remaining part. Card showing the west front, posted from Doncaster to London in August 1939.

51. Another view of the west front, this time on a Valentine's series card no. 22750. The estate descended in 1626 to the Yorkshire gentry family of Savile, one of whom, Lord Halifax, created an extremely long house by adding a new wing at the northern end.

52. Rufford from the north-west. The principal rooms were on the two middle floors, with servants' quarters and store-rooms in the attics and basement. The north and east wings were demolished in 1956. Card by Montgomery of Nottingham.

53. The second Lord Savile frequently held house parties at Rufford for notable guests. King Edward VII stayed here several times when attending Doncaster races. This card by George Ellis of Mansfield shows a royal group outside the Abbey in 1904.

COPYRIGHT

54. The clock tower, bell-cupola, entrance porch and ballustraded causeway leading to it, were the results of alterations made to the earlier buildings by Anthony Salvin in the 1830s and 1840s. Anonymously-published card bearing the date Easter 1914.

55. An anonymously-published card of the east front showing in the foreground one of many waterways designed and built since the 1680s as garden ornaments, and since destroyed with constant regularity.